Catch the Cookie

Written by Marcia Vaughan
Illustrated by Steven Mach

CHARACTERS

Man
Woman
Narrator
Bear
Moose
Fox
Turkey
Turtle
And the Cookie, of course!

■ CelebrationPress

An Imprint of ScottForesman
A Division of HarperCollinsPublishers

MAN: Looky, looky.
I baked a cookie.

WOMAN: It's big and it's sweet.
It's a cookie I'd like to eat.

COOKIE: Eat me, yes. Eat me, no.
You'll have to catch me.
Here I go!

NARRATOR: Away runs the woman.
Away runs the man.
They will catch that cookie
if they can.

COOKIE: I run high. I run low.

WOMAN: The cookie runs fast.

MAN: We run slow.

BEAR: Looky, looky.
There goes a cookie.
It's big and it's sweet.
It's a cookie I'd like to eat.

COOKIE: Eat me, yes. Eat me, no.
You'll have to catch me.
Here I go!

NARRATOR: Away run the bear and the woman and the man. They will catch that cookie if they can.

COOKIE: I run high. I run low.

BEAR: The cookie runs fast.

WOMAN, MAN

We run slow.

MOOSE: Looky, looky.
There goes a cookie.
It's big and it's sweet.
It's a cookie I'd like to eat.

COOKIE: Eat me, yes. Eat me, no.
You'll have to catch me.
Here I go!

NARRATOR: Away run the moose
and the bear and the
woman and the man.
They will catch that cookie
if they can.

COOKIE: I run high. I run low.

MOOSE: The cookie runs fast.

BEAR, WOMAN, MAN:
We run slow.

7

FOX: Looky, looky.
There goes a cookie.
It's big and it's sweet.
It's a cookie I'd like to eat.

COOKIE: Eat me, yes. Eat me, no.
You'll have to catch me.
Here I go!

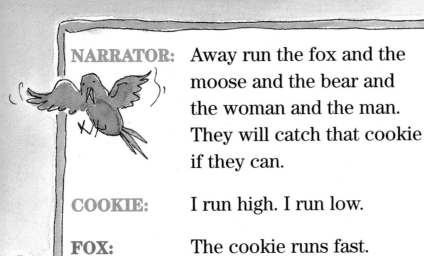

NARRATOR: Away run the fox and the moose and the bear and the woman and the man. They will catch that cookie if they can.

COOKIE: I run high. I run low.

FOX: The cookie runs fast.

MOOSE, BEAR, WOMAN, MAN:
We run slow.

TURKEY: Looky, looky.
There goes a cookie.
It's big and it's sweet.
It's a cookie I'd like to eat.

COOKIE: Eat me, yes. Eat me, no.
You'll have to catch me.
Here I go!

10

NARRATOR: Away run the turkey and the fox and the moose and the bear and the woman and the man. They will catch that cookie if they can.

COOKIE: I run high. I run low.

TURKEY: The cookie runs fast.

FOX, MOOSE, BEAR, WOMAN, MAN: We run slow.

TURTLE: Looky, looky.
There goes a cookie.
It's small and not very sweet.
It's a cookie
I do not want to eat.

COOKIE: Turtle, you are wrong.
I am sweet as can be.
Take a little nibble.
I am sure you'll agree.

NARRATOR: Turtle took a nibble there,
and he took a nibble here.
Turtle took so many nibbles,
he made that cookie disappear.
Up ran the animals
and looked around.
A fat, brown turtle
was all they found.

13

TURKEY:	Looky, looky.
	Did you see a cookie?
TURTLE:	Was it big?
OTHERS:	Yes!
TURTLE:	Was it sweet?
OTHERS:	Yes!

14

MOOSE: It was a cookie
we wanted to eat.

TURTLE: I am sorry.
You are too late.
That is the cookie
I just ate.

FOX: You caught the cookie?
It can't be true.
There is no animal
as slow as you!

TURTLE: My feet may be slow,
but my brain thinks fast.
I tricked the cookie
as it ran past.
But don't feel sad.
I'll mix up more dough.
We can bake lots of cookies
and let them all go.

16